OTHER PRINCIPAL CHARACTERS

DANIEL SHETLER
MEREDITH POTTER-BOLDT
THE MOON
ROGER WEINGARTEN

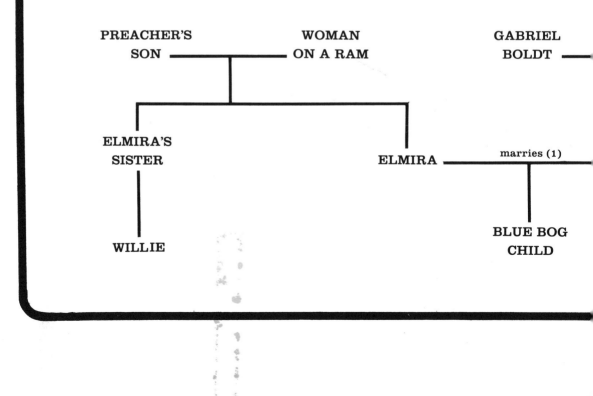

ARTHUR
MARGARET ——

PREACHER'S   WOMAN   GABRIEL
SON ——————————— ON A RAM   BOLDT ——

ELMIRA'S
SISTER   ELMIRA ——— marries (1)

WILLIE   BLUE BOG
CHILD

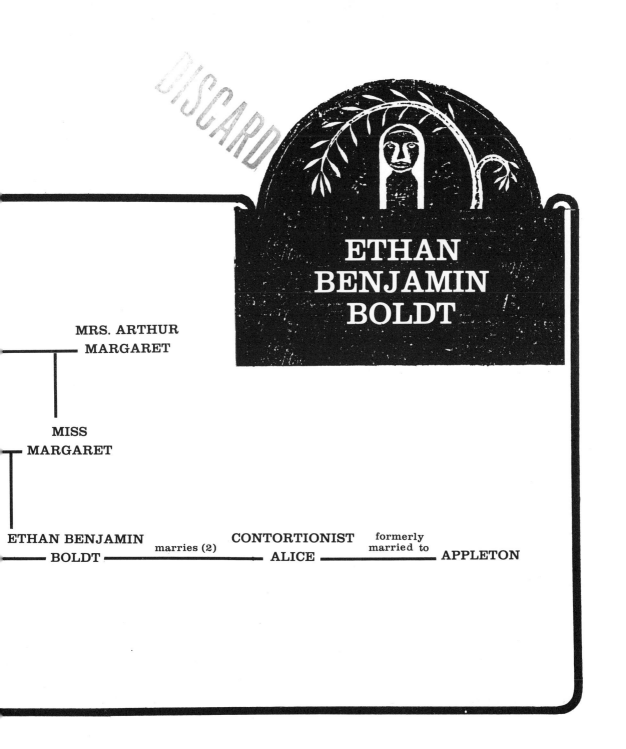

ETHAN BENJAMIN BOLDT

MRS. ARTHUR
MARGARET

MISS
MARGARET

ETHAN BENJAMIN
BOLDT ——— marries (2) ——— CONTORTIONIST
ALICE ——— formerly married to ——— APPLETON

ETHAN BENJAMIN BOLDT

Poems by
Roger Weingarten

ALFRED A. KNOPF · NEW YORK
1975

THIS IS A BORZOI BOOK
PUBLISHED BY ALFRED A. KNOPF, INC.

Copyright © 1975 by Roger Weingarten

All rights reserved under International and Pan-American Copyright Conventions. Published in the United States by Alfred A. Knopf, Inc., New York, and simultaneously in Canada by Random House of Canada Limited, Toronto. Distributed by Random House, Inc., New York.

"Blue Bog Children" and "Her apron through the trees" were first published in *Antaeus*.

"Ethan's Father's Poem" appeared in *rune* as "Gabriel Boldt's Narrative."

"A No-Nonsense Portrait of Meredith Potter Boldt" appeared in *The Clamville Collection*.

"These Obituaries of Rattlesnakes Being Eaten by the Hogs" appeared in *The First Annual Pig Farmers' Almanac*.

Library of Congress Cataloging in Publication Data

Weingarten, Roger.
    Ethan Benjamin Boldt.
    I. Title.
PS3573.E3957E8   811'.5'4   74-21328
ISBN 0-394-49456-3
ISBN 0-394-73047-X pbk.

Manufactured in the United States of America
First Edition

For my mother
and father

Acknowledgments

Certain pages are dedicated to: Kit and Roger Boldt (page 3),
Herbert Scott (page 9), Ronald Gatt (page 18),
Norman E. Dubie (page 21), Jon Anderson (page 40),
Bill Brown (pages 58‒59), Jeff Weingarten (pages 60‒61),
and Dina Yellen (pages 63‒64).

Contents

Ethan's Soliloquy

Ethan Boldt

In canary grass insects
fly around my head like quicksilver. I'm a pony-
express rider balancing a message
on foot, through weeds, over the sagging
barbed wire fence and a creek
to a graveyard.

I came West before I understood wild plants;
my reasons were good: twenty-three, leaning against
a brick warehouse, I saw the sky reflected
in the veins of my forearms, a rider paddling
a canoe through clouds, dark clouds. Father named me

Ethan after a book he never read; Benjamin
for the father of electricity. Mother sold
undergarments in a dry-goods store. She left
the eighteenth year in our stone house, her bosom
stuffed with cash, with a man who sold bone meal and bitters.

Doctor broke the bag of waters. Father stood
timing her contractions as she exhaled and sucked air
to get rid of me. Her belly folded. My brewing done,
Father laughed while I thundered

in his arms. I ate my food
with a little dirt, built my wife a shelter
by the Hocking River, left her
with a knife and blanket;

came back in the rain to a garden dug
with a clamshell, a son, and a wife about to die; grateful
I built the lean-to, our family

eating the skin of the wild turkey baked in mud;
I hate gardens, rivers are for fish. Bathe
in the rain when your body gets smoky! Outside
my bedroll in the weeds, my arms
paddle into a field of lightning.

The Offering

To see him crack a walnut without gloves,
without fear of the stain or his mother's
eight-pound iron, rip seams like an axe
fresh from the stone, and take the bark of a tree
off the head of a walnut caterpillar. Dan
Shetler spat tobacco in a blacksmith's forge;
of nine children, the only one without a nickname.
Blacksmith, beekeeper: through a pane of glass
I see his bellows no longer leather
but weathered dust
cursing me to pass on to the general store,
keep away from Dan Shetler's.

We ran. The woman he didn't marry
(I watched her stand away from beehives,
next to craters burnt white on the flesh
of his forearms) I buried
in a riverbed with cattails, her dress
weighted down with rocks, breasts as large
as the head of my son, heavy as a blacksmith's
anvil. Turn away from the window, Ethan.
There's nothing left of this town but the well.

Blue Bog Children

The remains of blue bog children
are fast clouds and no water; fat
trees without sap or bark; potato whistles
for the parson to pipe on—abrupt
and erupting—empty cisterns
of withered leaves breaking into light,

pornography read aloud in a wood known
for blue mosquitoes, blossoms that sail
and press under the shoes of children,
as the sleeves of a bridesmaid catch
on the pew. On red moss under ice, a bluebell

bog child, asleep, outside
a river town in western Illinois. His eyes
the size of fists, his wrists wound with briar,
banished by a storm that overflowed the river
for a fling with the shrubs. Strike the child

for kindling and hand him to a winter fire
to climb like field mice fingered in the hollow
of a tree, ashes poured into a wooden bowl,
the approach of a coffin on the horizon
of a trail, whispering children
riding to burial on their father's sled.

Skinny Dipping in Lake Apocrypha

From the wooden peg on a mud shack to a thorn.
Among strawberry runners and guinea tracks.
Lake Apocrypha applauds a wood pussy plié
on the violin-shaped petticoat
of a spit bug. Against a wax bean
pinned between her teeth, the squash-
vine lady spits up the Monongahela. Her wig

a rag, moccasins the soft green
cow pie of West Virginia. Her head shaved
with Revelations, her legs with cattails. Once over
a saucer of apple pandowdy, she said Grandpa
Elias invented the sewing machine because fat
Cousin Daniel was running the missus around
the clothesline under the horse blanket.

Run-In with a Priest on a Tyrian Beach around 850 B.C.:
What Ethan Did after He Fell Asleep during a Sermon

"I bowed; kissed his feet," and I
kissed the preacher who proved

that the shittim boards Noah
cut to build a ship were tongue

and grooved to give the Iroquois
something to hunt besides

the bear, give a sailor's
chance to families

of small quadrupeds. "Ahoy, Ethan,
grab my tail. I'm not a lamb

in captain's pants; I'm not
that deep. I only ask that you

purple the lips of the man
who breathed into the sails

and animals of the ark I lied about
to a scribe who had a wet

clay tablet and nothing to write."

Speech to an Eagle Falling to His Death

Your beak is chipped. Wings that beat
toward the gaze of mountain goats
are frayed. You can't see the brown
children of the pines turning in the wind

away from the oak your claws
grind toward sunrise, where red
clouds page everyone antique,
quiet, and strolling in undress
about the garden, and you answer:

fox grape is a red tail and purple eye.
give the raccoon someone to chase in late
October when the moon skates around the snow,
eyes hot as a pot-belly stove; her light
as cold as Cleopatra's Needle. And you're pinned

on the gnarl of a fallen oak, on a rise, observed
all at once and from all around; you wear
the leather of trees for boots. Ethan
Benjamin Boldt, I've come to feed you.

Ethan's Soliloquy

Coventry Patmore is a wholesome man
as I have ever met. You might
find him tying a woman's arms
around a linden tree, mockingly,
listening to her free-verse

strain of the *café concert*. You might
find him holding forth to a gentleman
on a country thoroughfare insisting that he once
lived with a beehive on his back for a diet
of wild honey, while the other hand

tucks a pistol and gold coins
into his skirts. Coventry Patmore
is a poet. His first book
is available at the Newgate Prison
and in the Boston Harbor. He has appeared

on handbills, in newspapers, including
the *Vermont Cynic*, the Pittsburgh *Post*,
and the Cleveland *Plain Dealer*.
He's captured the respect of other poets,
and there's a price on his head of five thousand.

Patmore's poetry leaves me wracked
with the seven jealousies. I agree
with his first poem: " . . . certain old woods
are sawdust, still have to be described,
nothing changes much, the bones of preachers

feed the earth." Although he's lying
mortally wounded under my foot, as long
as Coventry Patmore is healthy, writing,
and running off somewhere, I'll be happy.
Consider this poem his last word.

Her apron
through the trees

An Altogether Pleasant Pastoral

She lowered his eyes to her waist
but they surged like goats cropping
needles from a spruce tree, a goatherd:
his flock at the crossroads,

her muslin
dress thrown back from where
he knotted his calluses into the burs
snug in the hair of sheepdogs

and naked brats. She caught his beard
the way a bat nails a moth: with night
between its teeth, and on the wing.
With the first Methodist hymn in her throat,

and the battle dress of a storm beating laundry,
nearly overrun by a cavalcade of domestic
spillings and flies, she made the rain
rise in her mouth, spat it out for the swine.

Where Those Who Are Found Say There Is No One

The millshadow and the stiff
hemlock needles fall from the windrow and off the barn. Starling
eggs nest in the eaves of a house from which I'm seen overlapping

with shingles on a crossbeam. But my thoughts
are pecking at a window sash and a solitary
kettle in the yard, a woman riding an old ram in circles,
east of the barn, backward, with his tail in hand. This

sorceress should be taken from behind deep shrubbery or undergrowth.
Mosquitoes for eyes, thorns for fingernails, she watches my
industry through her hair, gathering
laughter in her throat around a fairy ring of ram
entrails. She dealt the preacher such a topper with the map

of Palestine, he passed through Samaria, but
for a gentle speech she married his son,

a sea-beast with the breath of a crab, the flesh of a leech, foaming

politely into a cloth in the first pew of his father's parish.
Elmira flows under the bridge of this swine. A wine with
natural underground connections, she moves behind the dark side
        of a window.
If evening ever comes and I'm around, she'll throw blankets over the gate,
search out a rock to support my head, throw her breasts at me, listening

through cornstalks for a windmill groaning at the heavens.
Revenge on half this daydream if she doesn't bring boiled
eggs:
exchange for steady courtship, no broken shingles, or my affection.

His Belt Was Made of Bark
and He Was Favourably Received

Ethan Boldt is at the door. His eyes are red.
Beyond the orchard his palomino Clyde
is in the locoweed. Ethan on the porch
is here to court with a wild bouquet. His eyes
are sleighs going their several ways, glittering

sisters buried in the door handle.
When my folks were killed in a press of trees,
we were in the milk house separating cream,
and through this peep-hole I built against thieves,
I hate him.

the gardeners war lovers peace

ethan your face turns
into a cluster of grapes

I wandered into your summer kitchen.
you were nervous *The gooseberry fool*

I bruised and boiled I left for you.
consider cambridge and the drapery

business *Imagine animals that taste*
you find your flavor an orange. tear out

the vineyard and the love affair
Because you rhyme

everything with orange I just
look at you leaving our bed

of asparagus for a feather pillow
The winters scattered your family

and your friends, you tore off my clothes
will turn you yellow, make you hard.

cover my eyes with topsoil *Why say*
that you will never understand? muscles

pushed thorns through my pores *They did not*
i won't leave you *But they did.*

Elmira's Nightmare

Gypsy camps and shop-windows came near
and nearer still, as if an avalanche of bees
above a river of wild mustard pinned me down,
sleeping face up beneath the moon.

The hairs on my body were the mustard plants:
the mosquitoes that landed there, the bees—

swarm around the navel, ignore the nose;
blood bubbles up from all the pores. Flood
without a storm, mosquitoes are oil wells,
anteaters worm their way into my lungs. My eyes

once eyed the wide lea, now they fill before a dam
of wings, my navel now a bath
for tired invaders. Gypsies camp
in shop-windows. The earth is cool.

Turns of Colic

The first sabbath night of another month. O God,
my breasts are pain, my week-old Willie is next to me
gumming spoonfuls of arrowroot (we're both

short on milk) and the Reverend Mr. Henry, your favorite
preacher, paid us a visit, forgot his cheaters,

brought up our mail. He beseeches me to meditate daily
and systematically. The anxiety these little ones
bring their parents. My nipples are very open.

I swore, but the preacher's store teeth smiled
so, I thought pain would disappear. A letter

from beloved Elmira
appeared among the bills. Nailed to trees
it stinks of pine. The letter itself is the corpse.

How I wish I could see her
in the world once more. Dear Sister. She's expecting

something. How am I supposed to read this? Mr.
Henry's found a wet nurse for me. How highly we are

distinguished from the poor. God I beseech thee,
provide for Willie's infant years, convert her husband.

An Hour of Music

A barn rat rises from powder under the loft.
His snout is soft, grey and lusterless. A coat
of beige with violet sleeves, he snakes through

the circle of Greek flowerpots and statuary.
In his left paw, a scroll casts shadows
into a palm branch between his teeth; around his neck

a silver chain, complete with ivory vessel
for incense and a crucifix. Opposite, an arched
window opens to the moon, illuminates a music-stool

adorned by crimson cloth, an hourglass,
cut crystal and a block of rosewood. A viola
da gamba leans against the bed, a four-poster

surrounded by a vase of potpourri, an emerald silk-
covered dais, a marble table, a reading lamp
for illuminated manuscripts. When he awakes

at twenty-six, the Society of St. George applauds
his sermon to away with war. His friends are St. Ursula's
flower and virgins. Ethan Boldt, passing through,

bending at the knee, while his wife in her powder-blue
gingham churns a bowl of cream, cocks
the hammer of his pepperbox. Into buttermilk.

Her apron through the trees

of the Elmira Wood
is a path overgrown
with gooseberry, King
Solomon's Gold, the dry

skin of the shagbark hickory.
It's late fall, late morning,
and we duck the cold
the way a slug fingers its way

into the gills of a honey mushroom.
Aboveground the brown leaves
and furry shafts of poison ivy
won't bruise your hands. Hand me

that hickory nut, her hard breast,
and everywhere we step the butternuts
are the stillborn spread around the jack-
in-the-pulpit, upon

the wet carpeting of the Elmira Wood.
Beneath stinkhorns a woman spins
the brown threads of the nineteenth
century; because of the ministry
of corn spiders, a few trees, and our walk,

she's not dead: we clean our fingernails
on her webs, the morning dew rising
from her wash-bowl. A stonecutter, in 1858,
chiseled a pig into her stone. She died
"of malaria." Elmira would.

Ethan's Father's Poem

Why Jack, whose children perished, who Suffered innocently, suddenly disappeared

For Michael Duke of Richmond

Your Grace, in March, 1792, the remains of one Jack
Toilet, of Thanesbury, were taken up, without permission,
from the dingle behind the cathedral mortuary.
Coffins
torn, monuments ransacked, a shrine

demolished: these intricate affairs, My Lord,
cross swords with the times, as the dignity
of the Church and Jack's blood mingle and carry
him on his way to matins. Another particular:
a labourer, a certain Arthur Margaret, an American of notorious

principles, claims he unearthed a cadaver
with an inscription carved into the flesh
around the neck. It reads: "Her piss smacks
of vinegar; Jack Toilet is not far." This will not
sit easily with His Grace, for a leg

of lamb and a silver tankard we should marshal his affection.
As for the remains of Toilet, there is a plot
for his children, a stone for his epitaph: "The fruit
of his generosity covered thirty acres; he took it with him, but
some, say the Egyptians, void their treasures on the run."

A Family Portrait

Mrs. Arthur Margaret, of Boston, with customary
tears began to wrestle her husband's memory
from her skirts. He molested an urchin, made
for England, and left her to the uncertain
poisons of starvation, public opinion on both sides,
and Mr. Gabriel Boldt pursuing their daughter,
speaking to her of solitude, how it turns a soft
bosom to burlap, green eyes to crochet needles and books
about religion. An urgent ceremony for Miss Margaret
and Boldt, a marksman who could hear his mother-
in-law's counsel box his eardrums as he marched.

Mr. Arthur Margaret, now of London, then a graverobber,
now a smuggler, the keeper of a pub, kept
contraband goods under the slats of his kitchen floor.
In the room above, in a dream,
he saw his wife razor the throat of a nanny goat. He lived
to a mellow thirty-four, peddling spirits, hot candelabra,
and cadavers in their prime. At the gallows with his hands
tied above his rump, the bow on a Christmas package, Saint
Nicholas hung from a thread of pop-corn and cranberries.
Mr. Margaret was shipped to Boston to be interred.

Gabriel, My Father

You loved an albino girl swimming in the river, fast peddlers
of a goodly wine administering their sacraments from booths

of tobacco smoke behind the dry-goods store, and tied Mother
to the topmost branch of a locust tree; thrust the root

of an evening primrose in her ear so she would overlook
an attempt to feed me to a dam bear. You left behind

a parcel of scalp in a pistol accident,
can peel your wig like a sheet of dried apricot

to entertain children who stick
fingers in the mustard bowl. You'd clean your bowels

with your nose if it were long enough, and you could
do it like a bat from the sign over the shop-window,

a cluster of grapes in bare feet. Father,
if one let go we would all be scattered.

Gabriel in Early Winter

His back arched into a fish-hook, the sharp nose
hung with bifocals above a weathered map.
Through a glass he overlooked the puddle duck
compelled to dabble in a cold pantry, the cock pheasant

making for the thicket. A mark he left
on the easy chair was not unlike one two eggs
impress upon their nest, a comparison for the trapper
and weasel caught by a storm between seasons

and out of breath. For weeks he swore to take a walk;
his thoughts were made of leaves; he fell on them
the way the Irenaki went to bed, not to fall asleep
but to end a civilization, the gait of the male praying

mantis looking over his shoulder but walking toward his mate.
It is fit that he be buried here: no brambles or moonlight,
cramped and unflattered, not the healthiest of men,
armed only with a familiar shadow and a cane. O nurse

of little faith, you flew to the dooryard for a dozen
turns with Gabriel, who scraped through the snow
in slippers, the genius of the storm.

Ethan's Father's Poem

I traded my overalls and work shoes for a loincloth and moccasins. I tied a band of cloth around my head, above my ears. I put on a beaded vest, then lost myself in a long line of Irenaki waiting for two Indians from a rival tribe to be untied to run the gauntlet.

They were fast but we nearly killed them. We feasted on venison, rubbed them with pitch, cut out their tongues, took their scalps, and set them ablaze. Their groan lasted only a few minutes.

Witwatweh led Rachel and me to his wigwam. Immense compared to the others, it was made of birch bark and painted in a fantastic manner. Strings of teeth, foxtails, antlers, and spears hung around the wall. The floor was covered with animal hides. Toolulu stood to greet her husband.

He addressed her this way: "Toolulu, wife of Witwatweh, chief of the Irenaki, you have wept too long over our son Highheel. He has gone to the hunting grounds I will go to. His sister keeps a fire for him. Lift your eyes and fix them on this son of the white man, for he is now our son. Look to this girl, for she has become our daughter. Take this brave, and this white-faced girl; give them space where we sleep; show them our ways; make them Irenaki."

As her eyes fell on Rachel, Toolulu groaned the sound of her own name. She turned to me as a minister would to his congregation, as if he spoke for God and they were listening. I wasn't. I was looking at Rachel.

The row of corn I'd been working was about finished. I thought I could rest a moment from my morning chore and stare off into the hills of western Massachusetts. I was daydreaming of horses when I heard horses coming at me, saw the face of Indians, and felt my arms tremble to the handle of the hoe.

Three dismounted and tied my wrists hard behind my back. I looked down at the corn shoots to grit my teeth against the pain. But if you read Aunt Sarah's diary, where it says "Even though he was a man of fifteen,

Gabriel wept aloud," you might ask her how she came to know that. I looked up to see if any of the Indians were watching my face. One was. He pointed to the yellow mouth painted beneath his chin. It told me he knew what I was struggling with. I looked away to see a squirrel run off.

I hunted most days with the men, spending my evenings with my stepparents and Rachel. Some days Toolulu would take the two of us for walks and teach us the Irenaki tongue with the things of nature.

One morning she told Rachel to stay behind and find work with the other squaws, as her brother had with the braves. Rachel said she was feeling poorly that morning and couldn't she stay in the wigwam. Toolulu looked to Witwat-weh. He pointed to the door.

Rachel went outside to a group of women. Toolulu and I walked to the woods.

We came to a spring. An Indian tied me to a tree, another gathered wood for a fire, another cut venison and held a rope in his fist that bound my leg. Fat dripped into the flames, driving sparks into the air with a whiplike sound.

Another group walked into the clearing. They gave the Indian who held me by the rope silent greetings. They brought their captives to him: a frightened lad about nine years old, a white-haired old man, and a girl who made me want to wipe the grease from my face. The little one said his name was Immanuel.

After an hour we came to a clearing warmed by the late morning sun. We had been talking the Irenaki tongue, and I was chattering in the words I had mastered in less than two months, when Toolulu stopped in the middle of the clearing and told me to lie down on the pine needles, which surprised me, so I did what she wanted without question.

She removed the comb from her hair and let it drop to the ground. She told me she wanted me to become as great an Irenaki as Witwatweh. She told me to undress, and she undressed, chanting an Indian song I couldn't make sense of. *"Mow chow nut-pess sell/Peri mar-hole wett./Yog wa egen'/ Yog wa egeno."**

Here's what the old man said to me before they killed him: "My granddaughter and I were picking blueberries, and Immanuel, my grandson, was taken while tending a sawmill in the village where his folks live. Never seen a girl as brave as this one, but the boy's too young to show his stock, God bless 'em both, my poor ticker's about to bust from all this walking. And the smell of that damned carcass burning is enough to make a Christian man puke his insides. You take care of them. You hear?"

We came back to the wigwam to find Rachel shivering beneath a stone's weight of furs. She didn't recover with the evening's meal, and for two weeks Toolulu tended to her needs. Witwatweh didn't stop hunting, but Toolulu ended my bridal lessons.

The chief brought a medicine man and two old women into the wigwam. They chanted, danced, and gave Rachel smelly herb balls to ward off evil. At night they circled with torches. I stayed with Rachel through the worst of it, feeding her pigeon broth from a wooden spoon Witwatweh carved for her on the other side of the lake, and listened to her whisper the gospel.

She didn't fight. She didn't care about the shadow circling the feathers, then the beads and spears; but once she watched it circle the wall, and let it go when it passed some scalps. She said to them, "I shall go back to Jesus and stay there until my mother comes. When you get back home, tell her I'm waiting for her."

*"You look funny with your long hair streaming in the wind, and sailing on a snail's horn."

I woke with sun in my eyes and Irenaki hurrying around me. I looked for Rachel but saw only Indians stuffing jerked venison into a skin. Immanuel, the old man, and I were forced to our feet to walk between two braves on horseback.

We caught up with a group of Indians and Rachel in the middle of the day. There were so many around her I only recognized her about ten feet away. I saw her stumble as if she were going to faint; the chief saw this and leapt for her. He picked her up, and carried her in his arms, chanting softly until we came to a small stream: *"Ee nil Etuchi nek n'kilaskitopp/Ee nil Etuche nek n'kil ooskedjin."**

Someone dragged the old man's body away. The chief claimed Rachel and me for himself. He passed small objects among his tribe. Toolulu threw dark arms around Rachel, who showed no pleasure at Toolulu's gift, a dress of moose skin, trimmed with fox fur and beads. Witwatweh handed me a beaded vest. Most nights we slept between Witwatweh and Toolulu under bearskins.

The braves were eager to go off in the snow to raid and hunt for game; a few stayed behind to guard the women and old men. We headed south for three days, barely keeping fed or warm, and when we came upon a small village, we were hungry.

Some were lucky and only driven off in the deep snow; most were slain; maybe ten were captured. I saw the medicine man's son throw a baby against a tree because it was crying. He made a prisoner of the mother while others grabbed arms of loot. They took anything: eight jugs of whiskey or eight pairs of skates.

Grief spread over the tribe. After Rachel's funeral even the medicine man was solemn. I became restless. I walked long in unfamiliar woods. Witwatweh

*"O, I am such a great man/O, I am such a great Indian."

told me that I might be taken, like his first son. He told me how his daughter had come crawling, half alive, to tell him Highheel was tied to a tree, his flesh burnt and torn by pine torches. He stared at me for a long time. He said if I tried to get back to my parents, "I'll take your cursed life and eat your liver."

We reached the southern end of Lake Champlain in two days. We brought out food and whiskey and began a small feast with a game for the captives, who were made to walk through a pit of hot coals, quickly and without sound.

My Indian brothers drank heavily, so it wasn't long before the shouting led to a general cry for me to show them how to use the skates. I said I would and all the pairs were snatched up. Those who got them went laughing and sprawling over each other on the ice.

I told them that if they wanted to learn they must take them off and let me choose the pair I wanted. To them this was great fun, so I managed to get theirs off and the best pair for myself. I secured these to my moccasins, begging them, for their own safety, not to put any on until they saw me do it.

They laughed at this, grabbed for the jugs, and I skated off.

I skated back and they cheered me. I thought of Rachel. I skated out again, widening into a circle, then skated in. They laughed harder, amazed at the skates, throwing their arms out to imitate my circles.

My circle widened and the foxtails in the wigwam went through my mind. I skated in and one of them looked at me suspiciously. He wasn't drunk like the rest. He grabbed a rifle and shouted to come back. I widened my circle.

The shouting turned to threats and loud curses. I felt the warmth of Toolulu's hands run through my legs, and widened my circle.

The sober one ran after me with a rifle. After a long chase, my skates gained on him. When he stopped to shoot, I thought I saw Toolulu's comb drop from her hair to the ground. A ball passed over my shoulder and I skated off toward the shore.

Masque

In the distance his eyebrows
are a network of fallen trees
and blackbirds, his eyes

the bare feet of women in organdy
digging herbs with knives
that uncover caterpillars

hunching in their green fluid
under berries of naked viburnum.
By moonlight his nostrils are large,

wet, and rotting within, each
a small bay surrounded by bulrush
on both sides of a low peninsula,

where a summer duck,
his upper lip, lays skinned and stuffed
with maggots that, like flies hung in dewlaps

from spider webs, turn
to the rhythm of an old woman's jaws
knitting an antimacassar to a hymn of dead solitude.

Alice's Epithalamion

Mothers Unwed
and Publicly Spoken to after the Rain

Her words rot outwardly over the platform, small
grass, and young women spreading corn bags
to stifle cohabitation of fishworms up for air

and meat loaves next to wicker baskets, under waistbands.
From a distance, in a mob-cap, a dowager
cups a hand to her nostril, dipping

into the scent as a goose is forced to swallow
mush to swell its innards, as if she nibbled raspberries
puffed with weevils that bit her lips. Our lady of the platform

speaks of girls scraping the beach to check starvation
under a crescent moon. Among a dozen men under an oak,
Ethan Boldt's lips move without sound, confined

by the bristles of his moustache, a tide pool in low
rocks and sand, his tongue towing a lobster toward the nursery
of men at his fingertips. To the women composed at the edge

of the common, his breakfast swimming in his throat, he testifies
that he would hawk them all through his canines,
into a bedpan, after he rogered a few more, and perished.

Contortionist Alice

Through my ankles I see brass stars
reflect my eyes on the lapels
of officers on leather-
stained blankets, my breasts
kneading into mud under vaporous

oil lamps. Acorns
fall on this tent and my husband
staggers in: a long
curved pipe, the bowl

carved in his image, steaming
on his jugular notch. He dreamed himself
into Moses with a thin
chisel sparking, or into the parting

of a sea locked
to a wandering moon
full of secrets not as fatal
as crossbars on the brown
epaulets of officers tugging

the reins strapped to my ankles. My fingers,
slithering like the pink
tail of a rat away from the urn
of your ancestors' ashes, welcome
the loss of that excuse.

Appleton's Mill

Let him love the military
music of cart wheels
rolling ground squirrels into road meal: and the war
of cornstalks against field pumpkins turning
into carrion when the moon's dead hand
drags his nightshirt from the buhrstone.
And if he suspects the bats
are circling more than water bugs, his hired men—
their eyes the red mud of foxholes—are milling
more than wheat, it's only that he calls

them as he sees them: he expects his wife's apron,
bearing chestnuts, not to puncture
on the burs. Her wish
that he were dead fills his whiskers with a victory
screech that diminishes with a wagonload
of furs beyond the well. Without her song,
more pumpkin than cornstalk, more
familiar than bats gliding off the paddlewheel
into the loft above a muskrat face
down in Appleton's Creek, he's not alone.

Changing Guard above Old Man's Ravine

Lost footing and sharp twigs jab the dew
out of your eyes. Your mahogany hands,
like paddles beating wild rice, smash
bark, leaves, and the yellow
deer mist on the snow into the creek.

Your eyelids are sparrow tongues
lapping the fluids of the wounded in bowls
of potato skins and milk, on the slopes
behind the pasture, a taste
of foot wrapping sliding down your cheeks.

Old man, this is life sticking her ankles
through the springs of a sofa, that frost-
bitten old cow swelling in the creek, your
father's clay-breasted lady, who would sever
her great toes to thicken your stew—easy

to harm, easy to cheat—a severe specialist
in holding: wet clothing over a flame, testicles
under a quilt, or her breath for a detachment
of cavalry riding through trees. Her braids
like grapevine sway in the leaves. A cart flies

up the New Road to her kitchen. A driver whistles
the alcohol of everyday life; his fingers
are blue jays robbing a nest, sticking out of his
gloves, strangling themselves in the reins
for warmth. Old man, this is life. You're relieved.

Ethan's Second Celebration

His contortionist bride planted his pocketknife
through his waistcoat into his side. Later
that afternoon she displayed

a wedding ring in her rabbit hutch. A weed
made its way through the ring
because a rabbit's needs are few and she left

the door open. His graveyard gives
no support to stones as weak as rabbit bones,
nor holds the pottery baked once

on the bonfire of his material possessions.
It is known for its red New Zealand rabbits,
not for the man who cantered

o'er his father's foot on a purebred Clyde,
with a belly hard from potato soup, a smile cold
from its own applause, and plighted his troth.

a three-legged stool

A No-Nonsense Portrait
of Meredith Potter Boldt

I

A border collie gums liver scraps
rotting with the vegetables.
Above the table, a crock

of comb honey and a basket
of chanterelles trade hands: an old beekeeper
straight as a ladder-back chair, fat as a hive,

and a young woman
who is not the devil in Massachusetts,
who speaks this Marketday evening with tidy

cousins and bulwarks
of the neighborhood circling the cherry
drop-leaf table. With marmalade

kittens against her foot, a songbook
on her lap, her eyes are penguins,
walk in snow, and when she passes

the fireplace with a brown pot, they see
her limp and hear the cold
tea slap against porcelain, moving patiently

toward the fractured wallpaper
of the servants cottage, where two
spinsters wear the celestial

calculations of organdy collars
and tortoise shell combs, rock
to sleep with crossed forearms

that frame withered
herbal charms, and the usual
connections of orphans and twins.

II

The self-portrait of the war between the states
is the daughter of my right hand being strangled
by her mother on Christmas Saturday, 1867.
That I might speak more than words

of braids and linen, not bake bread
for neighbors who applaud my
father on horseback in white suspenders,
or pluck that rude Connecticut fiddle

on a three-legged stool near the fire. The bird
is dressed and stuffed with figs. After punch
we wipe our mouths with family towels fastened
to servants who walk around the table

until it's Easter wailing and the tumult
of a Christian festival. A Smyrna
steamer anchored in the harbor, rising
on brown water, is a craft so modestly

graceful it's afflictive: waves
brush the sides and scrape the beach.
Villagers fuss at resort hotels
everywhere above the construction

of Virginia creeper and wild violets. War
between the states is what I want to stuff
into the little balls of rice we ladies eat
with the men who sit at table as missionaries

praying over the precious
females of this place to pass the cream
for their dreadfully unbroken lives,
and what remains is for the servants.

III *The Charnel House of Parma, Ohio*

This flight of stairs into the convent cellar.
The niches in the walls

are large enough for a nun
to stand baked and wearing a hood. A lamp

reflects a double sunset on vessels
of holy water in the marble

saddlebags of a donkey privileged
to carry a saint

under the Cuyahoga Valley with a scroll
or bedroll chiseled between her shoulder blades.

Across her untarnished hands
a garment worn by the limitless

and fatal Ursula. On the mossy breast
of a nun (her fingers festooned like vines

to intertwine with the next) a card
with her name, how many souls she's touched

by good works and prayer: her bones
painted with scriptural scenes,

and the streets of Jerusalem are narrow on the wrist
of Sister Hyginia, abolitionist.

That evening Roger
spent with the Boldts;
the next evening
they were gone.

Domestic Feelings

Toss a coin into the chimney
of a cave, between the boots
that stomached you from Boston

to this hill in southern Illinois.
Your feet are surgeons cutting
a throat that opens on a ripple

of animal tracks; take
this cave as home, your coin
as eviction papers that give you

the afternoon to swagger
in constant moisture, into a supper
of blind (recollect your wife's

sermon on childbirth) fish that trail
a stream of innards behind them, small
men with divining rods at odds with both

the water and their poles. Sharpen
yourself on a cave painting, trace the hag
with shoulders of fagots. Swear

this cave dweller would brush the misery
of man with a stalactite dipped
into his wives' monthly flow. Beneath

a natural bridge, near the crone
walking toward a fire that cracks and echoes
in the dream that closes with a child

about to pinch the flame on your last
half-a-candle, which you repulse with
a stutter, a coin flying out of your mouth.

Woman Looking at a Man through a Window
of the Reorganized Church of Jesus Christ

With a great rash of sun on my face
I walk before you in the middle distance
between two windmills
bringing up water for dairy cattle and two
black-and-lavender Amish families, the Borntregers
and the Beechys, who sell brown eggs
and Transparent apples and drive black cars.

On the other side of the road, as a child,
I learned to walk slowly. In the country
I want to bend
over the roadbed toward a pheasant and her brood,
but this is winter and the sumac
teases its red spears into the blue
belly of an afternoon that naps on white percale.

As if I were torn by disease-carrying beetles,
my clothes stripped like elm bark and fungus
blotching the remains, you look at me, and see
each rubbery step as your worst uncle's
favorite coon dog, his eye fixing
yours in one rural tragedy after another until
you become cold, religious, and mounted like eyes
on the impaled
wing of a butterfly under glass.

And

this poem is a barn raising itself above suspenders
with cobwebs for curtains, a farmer with a crocus-
bulb nose, his daughter's breasts, which is where
two barn swallows enter this poem, reaching

for a vein at the end of his nose to build
a nest or drop on the feverish cow who can't
make water on the spot. He explains distemper
to his Simonese cat. He tempted John Woods to read
and write poems made of refinements a man throwing

mice against a fever could afford, who swears his name
came about when an ancestor had his throat cut
with a conch under a whorehouse of palms in Polynesia.
And you haunt the next stanza like a footprint
and the reflection of a plank:

                              your nephew's son
tears down stalls, your daughter's funnel-
shaped vision above the silage of the complexion
of a Jehovah's Witness lipreading the feedbags
nailed over the gate that speak

"of continuing through warmer months and a deleterious
effect on the community." And even though elders
remove fecal matter, the partial bodies of puppies,
and spoil our party like county inspectors late for a meal,
I wrote this poem to cheer you, to say, Mr. Shellhouse
of south

western Michigan, I move in your elemental self. Nonetheless
we are both found suffering the malnutrition of old
folks about to clean house. Nevertheless, the barn,
like the lantern of a woman in labor fleeing the ceremony
in the evening rain, grows more visible than ever when we
were younger men and did the chores.

These Obituaries of Rattlesnakes Being Eaten by the Hogs

1

The arthritic farmer and a calf watch Dr. Graves
punch a needle into the jugular
of a cow with milkfever, and feed
calcium salts from a jar into a surgical tube. I wonder
at the flat maroon afterbirth of the night before, the farmer's
tobacco pouch, and the brown saliva of 6 a.m. on his lip.

In a booth at The Grill I order wheat
cakes and tea, the vet
a waffle and a tuna-fish sandwich. He shouldn't
tell me this but every time he looks up at the cookie-
punched tin ceiling he sees the farmer, his child stumbling
into the bailer, how he found her leg sticking out of the hay,
went home for his scattergun, and blew his brains into a burlap bag.

Standing in a manure gutter holding a heifer by the ears
over the wood slats of a manger, a farmer's wife, with sour
cream on her breath, asks what's my name, my business
in life, tells me that all this must be very
inspiring, and when the heifer's nose, clamped and tied to a beam, starts
to pull away from her face, I pass the tattooer, the syringe,
and the ink to the vet and say it is, Mrs. Hochstetler, it is.
"Then why don't you get out of the light so he can write the bill."

About two instruments with funny names: the twitch and White's
improved emasculator. The twitch is a bat with a loop tied at one end
you twist around a horse's nose that hypnotizes

while you run a lubricated tube down a nostril into the belly. Pump wormer
into the tube, warm water, and air. I
hold the twitch, while Doc tells his fingers, red from the cold
and white from the wormer, that horses
bring out the steel in women.

2

Chili and coffee at The Grill, and a walk through the Lower
Deer Creek Cemetery, granite table lamps, pink marble
urns, epitaphs with Old Testament first names, and bestial icons
get the Doc wondering if the Christians around here aren't a little
too much like the Egyptians and the Jews. He powders
their heads and tosses
testicles into a long glove that I hold open for our supper.
Horns and scrotums get lost in the straw, and barn cats
risk being trampled for a meal. Dr. Graves, after a twelve-
hour day, packing a testicle into a snowball that breaks against
the barn, tells me that the branches of a walnut tree in winter
are like the legs of a woman on a mattress of twigs, that dehorning
a bull sounds like cobs breaking.
That he once lay down with a woman under the axletree
of a cart just outside Lancaster, Pennsylvania, and when
we got home, if I would kindly peel the tunic
off the tripes, he could pour us a sly drink from the cider jug.

To Woodrow Miller

Like two men walking a Sunday meal
through pines after a fire, the isinglass
in your oven door cracked in its philosophy,
only the foundation resisting
this argument. Your children pack me off
to furnished rooms away from bedrooms

we occupied like cattle in a blizzard.
Wallpaper swings from the Dutch
ceiling like feedbags overlooking the ravine
where generations of Millers will marry
machinery to erosion and you embarrass me
speaking into the rotten arms

of a one-man plow. "When a poet
looks across the land, he sees
things a farmer doesn't see." Carolyn,
who sleeps with a pillow over her head,
wakes me to the objections of Brenneman's
midnight cigarette. I see poems
burning in the toaster, the hysteria of coffee

boiling for firemen, and Esther's eyes
moving us out. Last August, near the Russian
olive tree, you asked me to a gathering
of the Deer Creek Conservative Mennonite
Church. I refused like a farmer
on a willow branch over a gully, inhaling mucus
and sixty-mile-an-hour hail, pheasants

flying from the muck you quit plowing
for the reason I quit pounding a younger
Weingarten. His memory of childhood
follows your orange sweat
shirt into a blizzard
of Holsteins. The red arithmetic of a cow
washes off your hands. Your hired man,

Brenneman, swears that Jews have a real taste
for young pigs; his eyelids
cover satisfaction like lettuce over peas,
calls you Woody, exhaling news of a coronary
at the county home. I say
raise the rent, leave Brenneman to care
for the rationality of bullet holes in the tractor.

In front of the tractor, spelling with your finger
your wife's maiden name in the dirt
lane that leads to our black-shuttered house,
you lie back on the wild bed
near Esther's family pond, her red hair
the new ivy, the song in your story

an aluminum band punched into a heifer's ear
churning out the cream-faced Amish boy
who rode a courting buggy out of Illinois
over bundling boards and the high flame
of your father's excommunication in your mother's ear.

Neighbor

Between the rows of Stutsman's orchard
keeper-apples pyramid
under snow, under sheep bellies,
and an orange cat erasing bark with its claws.
A red frame house protected on three sides by a sixty-year-
old windbreak fed to the fireplace with a chain saw.

Its spine rises in native stone into smoke, warming
his busy widowed mother. Stutsman found her curled
under a wire fence, kept pressing cider
until mud season. A desk job in the city opened
near the Eagles' Club, where aluminum tables
horseshoe around his slow dance with a silver-haired

divorcee, and sister, a real-estate broker with a taste
for cognac and ginger ale, who takes the world as middle-
aged men, smooth as sweet rolls and alarm clocks, to feed
her desire for doors, roof, and a little
beast at the foot of the stairs, with an apple
core in his left hand, a pallbearer's grip on the banister.

Philosophy of Life with Fisherman

Believe the trees bordering the lake
circle a cold
philosophy of life, and you won't

believe an inch of that woman
near the cattails, a fish approaching
your fish hole, and that a severely

crazed uprooted tree is more than just
a winter sketch, detail-jammed by a turn-
of-the-century Sunday painter

whose inventory of the morning
is a sermon crisscrossing the wooden
furniture of the place and its inhabitants.

But this
is Sunday. The woman with mittens
skates out of a weeping

willow grove. At seventeen her philosophy
spoke of my long fingers, bad posture,
and I wrote her poems on onionskin. Her slides

of the Gothic architecture at Bruges,
husband falling
into "the filthy canal," and her

indifference to the silver eagle
with red light-bulb eyes
blinking in Otto

Moser's saloon, where vaudeville clippings
are lacquered to the walls under a fortune-
teller's parlor and her tea leaves.

Andersonville Insinuations

A prisoner-of-war-camp memory of being
carried through gates and spitting in the guard's eye,
fifty pounds lighter than when you walked in, spills out

under the "Truckers Only" sign. You compare the fat
rendering under the waitress's apron to February ice
on the Maumee. You lick malt off a steel shaker, blood

off a T-bone, and sermonize looking into the hams
of a waitress stacking dishes under the counter
as if she were a trailer off the road. Her ears

rear-view mirrors, she inquires
about snow in Defiance, whether
you need a double order of suicide to go. We pass

a table of fried potatoes and truckers' hands not slapping
knees at a round of sex jokes, the wall behind
selling fiesta, bullfight, and Last Supper towels.

And you're proud you support a mother, a five-bedroom house,
looking back at the circle pin framing the crucifix
at the neck of an apron, and walk the seventy percent of your body that

still functions past the cashier's bracelets, your rig
left running with headlights like white
vaccinations, passing through Ohio with hitchhiker.

Twister and the Vagabond Babbler

I ignore the spiderwort. I say ignore the moccasin track,
the harmless back of the brown-and-yellow spider,
the funnel that drops down around my bedroll,
and buries me in a mile's torn brush and ground,

currants, arrowheads, the stomach's demands, the narrow
look in the eye of a grey wolf. I consider
my position, consult the clouds. Morning,
and I dream I'm an ox, bloated and covered with flies,

pulling a buggy filled with Mother
into a bluebell bog where we grew up
hiding dried catalpa pods in our back pockets,
Elmira's pigtails in mine.

Whip me, frown, smooth back her hair.
Why don't you light tobacco, keep off the flies?

A NOTE ABOUT THE AUTHOR

Roger Weingarten was born in Cleveland, Ohio, in 1945. He was educated at Goddard College and the graduate school of the University of Iowa. In 1967, he directed the Young American Poetry Series at Expo '67 in Montreal. From 1970 to 1973, he taught English literature at Western Michigan University (in Kalamazoo). In 1973, he was awarded a Creative Writing Fellowship grant from the National Endowment for the Arts. He lives in East Montpelier, Vermont, with his wife, Dina Yellen, a ceramic sculptor.

A NOTE ON THE TYPE

The text of this book was set in film in a type face called Clarendon. The modern version of this face was designed by Hermann Eidenbenz and was issued by the Haas Type Foundry in Switzerland in 1952. However, the Eidenbenz designs were based on a nineteenth-century English type face of the same name. At that time the word Clarendon was generally used in England to describe square-serif faces.

The book was composed by Black Dot, Inc., Crystal Lake, Illinois; printed and bound by American Book—Stratford Press, Inc., New York, New York.

The book was designed by Earl Tidwell.